Simple Crow~~d~~

Learn the Secrets to Crowdfunding Success

By Davin Poonwassie and Atuksha Poonwassie

Copyright

Limit of Liability / Disclaimer of Warranty

The content contained herein provides an introduction to Crowdfunding and Peer to Peer Lending. It is not intended to be financial advice. The advice and strategies contained herein may not be suitable to your individual circumstances. Anyone considering investing or borrowing through a Crowdfunding platform should seek financial advice. The authors shall not accept any responsibility or liability for any damage, howsoever arising.

Whilst the authors believe that the content of this book to be accurate at the time of going to print, no warranty is given and no liability is accepted in the event of any errors.

Further information about the authors can be found at the back of this book.

Printed in the UK.

Table of Contents

Preface

Curious about Crowdfunding but don't know where to begin? This book provides a simple introduction to Crowdfunding. The aim of this book is to introduce the concept of Crowdfunding to everyone and how both Investors and Borrowers can make the most of this new, innovative marketplace.

Whilst we understand that Crowdfunding is relevant to global markets, the focus of this book is the UK market.

Our belief is that Crowdfunding and Peer to Peer Lending will become more mainstream and shall allow for increasingly innovative business ideas and property projects to be brought to market and completed. These are very exciting times!

Well done to you for exploring and seeking information on this new world of opportunity and finance. Already by doing so and by seeking new information and learning, you are giving yourself an edge over your competition. We hope the contents of this book can help open up new horizons and new options and alternatives for you, to increase further your prospects of a great future.

We wish you every success in exploring this new marketplace and hope that if you are looking to borrow money, your business ideas and property projects get funded successfully and that if you are looking to invest, you are able to invest in ideas that excite you and you are rewarded with good returns.

Acknowledgements

We are thankful to so many people who have helped us get this book to where it is today. Their insight, support and time has been instrumental in helping us shape the structure and content of this book.

In particular, we wish to thank Kevin Green and Dan Latto for giving us the guidance and support in growing our Crowdfunding business and Simon Speed for your help and encouragement in writing this book.

We also wish to extend our thanks to the Simple Backing team and our family, friends and clients who have been there every step of the way. Your support has been invaluable.

Why We're Writing This Book

"Right now, entrepreneurs are already using Crowdfunding to raise hundreds of thousands of dollars in pure donations – Imagine the possibilities if these small-dollar donors became investors with a stake in the venture." – President Barack Obama

Investing and borrowing money is a business that dates back many thousands of years. Despite the passage of time, the principle methods have changed very little. First there were money Lenders or Investors, and then banks. But the rules stayed pretty much the same. You borrow money and you pay it back plus interest. If the banks didn't want to lend you to, your idea usually fell to the cutting room floor. If you had money to lend, it was not terribly easy. You would need to ensure you had good legal contracts and evidence of the loan to protect you if the Borrower didn't pay it back.

This put off many people who could lend, with the result that they invested in savings accounts. These do not always reward the saver well, especially when interest rates are low (as now). Of course there are other ways to invest money; shares, bonds and so on, but if an Investor hears about a new and exciting project, until now it has not been easy to get involved, to help the project and to receive a decent return for doing so.

And there were the risks. Over the years we have all heard about bogus investment schemes, sometimes very ingenious, that have resulted in Investors losing out. Even now, different strategies for Investors are found and not all of them are safe.

With Crowdfunding, a new and exciting alternative has arisen, for both Investors and Borrowers. It is exciting because it casts off the mainstream shackles of the traditional and often unimaginative banking system and instead relies on the entrepreneurial vigour of our peers. If you have a great idea and your peers recognise that, you have a great chance of now being funded – even if the banks didn't previously want to help you.

And Investors can suddenly get involved in exciting new projects much more easily! Instead of personally lending direct to the Borrower, Investors have the reassurance of transacting through a Crowdfunding platform, with legal contracts in place to support them. There are regulations in place for Crowdfunding platforms that help control and monitor this marketplace.

The downside of Crowdfunding is that it is not that well known and understood. The purpose of this book therefore, is to help develop the Crowdfunding message and to help people like you to learn more about it. Crowdfunding may or may not be right for you, but a new way, a revolution in money transactions has begun, and that has simply got to be worth reading about!

Simple Crowdfunding Fact
The Neasden Temple in London - The temple has been a triumphant Crowdfunding example. A group of ordinary Londoners joined forces and using their faith, hard work and business nous pulled together the funding, land, materials and skills to build something spectacular.

What Is Crowdfunding?

"The idea of Crowdfunding is fundamentally based on social good, appealing to the shared interests and beliefs of the masses, seeking their support in campaign form."
– Amanda Barbara

The Financial Conduct Authority (FCA), who are the regulatory body in the UK, define Crowdfunding as this:

"Crowdfunding is a way which people, organisations and businesses (including business start-ups) can raise money through online portals (Crowdfunding platforms) to finance or re-finance their activities and enterprises."

The History Of Crowdfunding, Where It's Going And Why It Has A Future

The banking system is one of the vital institutions of the modern day which touches our lives in many ways during our day to day activities. Banking has been slowly evolved since ancient times when people first started to barter and trade for goods and services. Over time, Empires and religious institutions became places for storage of wealth, mostly in the form of gold. These wealth stores were taken care of on behalf of their owners, by a group of persons who acted as their custodians. Over time, this system became the foundations of the modern banking system.

What we would recognise as the banking system of today truly appeared in the 16th Century. At that time, cashiers in Amsterdam belonging to the trading and shipping industry undertook to keep safe valuables of others for a charge. This system of dealing with valuables and wealth came to UK after this time. These cashiers began to offer other services like paying money to 3rd parties on behalf of their customers, based on a written instruction which became the basis for the present cheque system.

British Banks began operating as fully fledged financial institutions during the latter part of the 17th Century. The next stage was pre-printed cheques that came into use in the 18th Century. A clearing system began functioning later where cheques of all banks were settled and cash paid according to their balances.

In the year 1778, the Royal Bank of Scotland introduced the overdraft feature, and the holding of a bank account which had already been a symbol of the rich, became a necessity for even the middle class households during the 19th and 20th Centuries. Today we have more than 10 banks in the UK that have been continuously working since the 17th Century.

Now the banks have become so important in our lives that we cannot conceive our life without a banking account. We use banks for our daily cash transactions and most of us receive our salaries, pension and other credits through our bank account only. We use our debit and credit cards as a way of spending money for our daily use. Having a bank account is a basic requirement.

Today our banks are offering many services and they have become one of our most essential institutions. Some banking functions can now be offered by alternative types of companies, including activities relating to Crowdfunding. This development of allowing Crowdfunding companies (or platforms) to lend money via Crowdfunding activities has opened up many ways to finance projects of all types and sizes and as such help individuals and businesses meet their financial aspirations in a systematic and easy way. We see that the concept of Crowdfunding is becoming a popular way of backing projects that have wide ramifications for a large number of people.

Crowdfunding has made it possible for large groups of people to come together to offer their joint economic power to support a project, functions of a company or an organisation to conduct its services or functions and in turn to bring their benefits to society.

What Can Be Achieved Through Crowdfunding?

Although Crowdfunding as a concept is still fairly new, it can be used wherever a group of people (the crowd) would like to support the main cause of the funding effort. For instance a fund that is collected to give relief to people affected by a disaster is a good example of a modern day Crowdfunding campaign.

Crowdfunding is a good way for raising funds for big projects or for implementing unique ideas that can benefit large numbers of people, bringing the dreams of innovative minds into reality. A Crowdfunding platform helps business owners, entrepreneurs and developers to put across their unique ideas to a large number of people. It brings a feeling of 'community' and this sense of belonging is used for financing even very large projects in a simple and voluntary way.

Crowdfunding can also help people who want to give their time and money for a noble or charitable cause. It is a way for the contributors to come together as a single entity and show their collective might in achieving great benefits. It is a good way to fund the day to day activities of non-profit organisations, entrepreneurs, individuals and groups of people who need funding for creative and beneficial projects. It can also work well for civic leaders who want to take new initiatives to help their schools and communities, and as such a wide variety of persons can benefit through Crowdfunding.

Crowdfunding is a special way of raising funds and finding the required level of financing for progressing your projects, products and services that might look interesting to many people. With the modern methods of communication such as social media, email, video, the ability to reach a vast number of people in an instant, starting and running a Crowdfunding campaign is quite easy. With possibilities for both online and offline promotion of the Crowdfunding activities, it is now possible to get a good response to your Crowdfunding efforts. As a result, we see that many of these campaigns and platforms are becoming more successful than ever.

Crowdfunding can be offered for start-up companies by way of paid membership subscriptions that gives Investors certain rights in the company or receive their products at lower rates in advance before the general public can. Crowdfunding is also a viable option for property developers to fund their projects, both smaller and larger with the promise of certain benefits to those who choose to invest.

The Crowdfunding Opportunity

Crowdfunding is a fast growing way of injecting finance into projects and start-ups that are looking for financial support for their activities. The growing popularity of emerging Crowdfunding platforms indicate that this industry is set for tremendous growth. There is no doubt that Crowdfunding is going to play a vital and significant role in the investment market.

Crowdfunding can be used for both start-up as well as established companies to implement their innovative and unique ideas if they offer benefits to a large enough 'crowd'. This type of funding is a very strong alternative to the conventional ways of financing through banks and venture capitalists. Whilst Crowdfunding is still considered to be in its infancy, it is developing into a strong offering. It is likely to become one of the most viable and easiest routes to funding, for even unusual projects that may otherwise struggle to raise finance.

It is possible to apply the benefits of Crowdfunding to specialist industries and groups such as musicians, publishers and software developers and niche, specialist Crowdfunding platforms are starting to emerge.

Crowdfunding projects can be flexible in their outlook. For example, a project might seek funding for its initial stages, then when completed, approach the Crowdfunding platform for continued funding for the remaining stages of the project. So long as the terms suit both the Borrowers and Investors (the crowd), the project can continue. This is especially relevant in the case of bringing products to market. Crowdfunding may be used to develop a prototype. Then, if the prototype appears to be a success, more funding can be sought to produce the prototype, ready for market sale.

Thus, Crowdfunding is a way of funding projects and services that are of interest to a large number of people. Its popularity is rising and the emergence of many Crowdfunding platforms will help the general public to find out about Crowdfunding and the opportunities that it presents.

The following figures show that Crowdfunding as a way of raising funds, is growing substantially in the UK. From 2012 to 2014, Loan based Crowdfunding (Peer to Peer Lending) has increased in the UK by 250 percent for business lending and 108 percent for consumer lending. Equity Crowdfunding has increased by 410 percent, Reward based Crowdfunding by 206 percent and Donation based crowdfunding by 77 percent. The market is set to top £4.4 Billion in 2015. – Understanding Alternative Finance 2014, Nesta.

Simple Crowdfunding Fact

Barack Obama - Crowdfunding in political campaigns became popular with President Obama's presidential bid in 2008, but it was his re-election campaign in 2011 that really displayed its power.

That year, 72 percent of Obama's fundraising total of $118.8 million was raised by donations of less than $1,000, and 48 percent came from donations of $200 or less.

Types Of Crowdfunding And How It Works

**"Perhaps Crowdfunding can help restore the magic by
freeing entrepreneurship from the taint of big finance." –
Reihan Salam**

We have seen that Crowdfunding is a recent and fast developing
opportunity for entrepreneurs and business owners to obtain funding
for their projects and for Investors to obtain higher return on their
money than traditional options may offer.   But who else can benefit
from involving themselves in Crowdfunding and what types of
Crowdfunding are there?

In essence, there are four main types of Crowdfunding.   A
Crowdfunding platform may combine one or more of the four types or
they may solely concentrate on one type. Indeed, some Crowdfunding
platforms may niche further and only offer investment opportunities in
one area of business. The four types of Crowdfunding are:

Equity Based Crowdfunding

This type is defined by what the Investor receives in return for their
investment – Equity.   Equity means a share of the company or
business, and/or of the profits generated by the business. A new or
established business or company may seek Crowdfunding for a
variety of reasons and in return, offer to the 'crowd', an equity stake in
the company.

In this way, the Investor obtains a part ownership stake in the
company. If the company, perhaps by good use of the funding
received, goes on to be successful and increases its value, so the
Investor's share in that company will also grow in value. Ultimately, it

is up to the Borrower to decide what they will offer to Investors and for the Investors to decide if what is offered is attractive enough for them to invest.

So how is this type of Crowdfunding different to the traditional method of buying and selling shares in a company? In some respects, there may not be many differences. However, this method of Crowdfunding allows business owners to offer a stake in their company, and to do it through a Crowdfunding platform that advertises the deal to the general public. Previously, it was much more difficult for a company to do this. A large Limited company listed on the Stock Exchange could manage a share based fundraising scheme, but relatively few companies are in that position.

The Investor must check the details of the offer, to ensure it suits what they want to achieve. The Investor should be aware of the risks that are associated with taking on an equity stake in a company. If the company goes on to perform badly or even to cease trading, the share in the company may become worthless. Check that the potential rewards justify the potential risks.

Sometimes, the Investor can do no better than to make an educated guess on the company's future performance. They should check how the company is set up, the strengths of the management team and the business plan. If these elements look ill prepared, ill thought out or ill qualified, the Investor may well be wise to stay away. All of these pieces of information should be available for potential Investors via the Crowdfunding platform, who should have received them from the Borrowers when they submitted their project for Crowdfunding. Remember to always take advice before making an investment, especially if you intend to invest a significant sum of money.

In the UK, Equity based Crowdfunding raised an average amount of £199,095 per project and two thirds of investors invested more than £1,000 – Nesta. An example of an Equity based platform is 'Crowdfunder'.

Rewards Based Crowdfunding

This type of Crowdfunding is characterised by the Borrower offering to supply a reward in return for an investment. What could the reward be? Well virtually anything!

This type of Crowdfunding is often used in the so called grass-roots projects such as a new company intending to launch a new product or service. Crowdfunding platforms like Kickstarter specialise in this area.

Often, the individual payments from Investors will be fairly low, perhaps between £10 and £100, but collectively, the sheer number of investments (pledges) mean that the project receives high levels of funding. These types of projects might be to produce a piece of clothing, to open a gym or to publish a book. The Investor may receive the produced item free or at a discount, receive a reduced membership fee or simply reserve the right to buy the item earlier than the rest of the market.

This type of Crowdfunding has really taken off and is highly popular. Generally speaking, the more radical and innovative a new product or service is, the more likely it will grab the Investors' attention and receive the funding the project needs.

Rewards based Crowdfunding projects in the UK raise an average of £3,766 per project with the majority of Investors spending less than

£50 on supporting projects – Nesta. An example of a Rewards based platform is 'Kickstarter'.

Loan Based Crowdfunding (Also Known as Peer To Peer Lending)

In this type, the Investors provide funds on a loan basis and receive the original loaned sum back at the end of the term (or at least should receive it back) as well as an agreed rate of interest that is paid either at regular intervals or at the end of the term. The rate of interest may well be higher than is currently being offered by more traditional savings routes, such as banks savings accounts or bonds. This type is especially prevalent in the property investor and developer world.

Loan based Crowdfunding projects in the UK raise an average of £73,222 per project for business lending and £5,471 per project for consumer lending. For business lending, 33 percent of borrowers believed that they would not get the funds elsewhere. For consumer lending, 54 percent of investors have lent more than £5,000 – Nesta. An example of a Loan based Crowdfunding platform is 'Simple Backing'.

Donation Based Crowdfunding

Here, people or companies invite the 'crowd' to help with their activity, whatever that may be. Usually, no return is offered and thus is the most philanthropic of all 4 types of Crowdfunding.

The types of activity can be as wide ranging as anything funds might be needed for! From securing donations sought for a person to do or achieve something, to large community projects or fundraising and charitable initiatives. In many ways, charitable giving has always been a type of Crowdfunding. The difference here is that the Borrower does not need to be a registered charity and can broadcast their request on a much wider scale very quickly.

Whether or not the donation based project receives funding will depend on the merits of the project itself. Excellent charitable projects to help a noble cause may well receive large amounts of donations regardless of the size of the project. It could be a wheelchair for an amputee or a new music hall for a school or a relief fund for recent disaster. The opportunity for charities and other good causes to raise funds is substantial.

The average Donation based Crowdfunding project in the UK raises £6,102 per project. In addition to this, 27 percent of donors had offered to help or volunteer with the project they backed – Nesta. An example of a Donation based platform is 'JustGiving'.

How Does Crowdfunding Work?

We have talked about the 4 main types of crowdfunding so let's now look at some of the terminology and how Crowdfunding works in practice.

Crowdfunding platforms are like a 'matchmaker'. They typically have online presence and advertise for Investors and Borrowers. The online trading site is known as the Crowdfunding platform.

Borrowers approach the Crowdfunding platform, register and then discuss the opportunity to list their project on the platform. If accepted, the Borrower shall invite 'pledges' from potential Investors. A pledge is a notification from an Investor that they intend to invest in the project. It should be noted that a pledge does not commit the Investor to invest at this time. An Investor can cancel or revoke their pledge but it is hoped that this is not the case. Crowdfunding platforms will monitor this type of activity and if Investors pledge and do not invest, there is a good chance that their ability to pledge will be limited over time.

The Borrower will have set a funding target that they are seeking to raise to get the project off the ground. If the target amount is not reached, the project is deemed to have not succeeded and the pledges from all Investors will be cancelled. The full amount has to be pledged in order for a Crowdfund project to go ahead.

If the funding target is reached, the Investors who made a pledge shall be informed and asked to make a payment of the pledged amount to the Crowdfunding platform. The platform shall administrate and record the payments received from the Investors, as well as the individual terms of the pledge and then release the investment monies (less the platform fees) to the Borrower. Note, the fee the platform charges can vary from 2% upwards of the total investment. This fee is typically payable by the Borrower.

The platform shall then administer the collections of payments from the Borrower and distribute payments or shares to the Investors. It should be noted that for some rewards based Crowdfunding projects, the reward may be sent directly from the Borrower to the Investor without further intervention from the platform.

Simple Crowdfunding Fact

Crowdfunding is older than the Statue of Liberty in New York -- which incidentally needed Crowdfunding from the American and French people.

Crowdfunding Regulations

"The power of the people is stronger than the power in people." – Bono

Many countries are embracing the opportunity that Crowdfunding brings. These include the UK, US, most of Europe, China, Australia, New Zealand, India, United Arab Emirates, Sweden, Israel, Canada and many others. The regulations vary from country to country, and some countries are more heavily regulated than others. Here, we provide a brief introduction to the UK, US and Europe. Details of these organisation can be found in the Resources section of this book.

United Kingdom

One of the first Loan based Crowdfunding platforms to operate in the UK was 'Zopa', founded in February 2005. It is now the largest Loan Based Crowdfunding platform in the UK. Many platforms have since emerged, many growing to a significant size.

The Crowdfunding industry is better regulated today and certain types of Crowdfunding such as Loan based or Equity based are carefully monitored activities. Since April 2014, the Financial Conduct Authority (FCA) has taken over the regulation of this market in the UK. Their goal is to help consumers get a fair deal by making sure the financial markets work well. This means ensuring:

1 - The financial industry is run with integrity
2 - Firms provide consumers with appropriate products and services
3 - Consumers can trust that firms have their best interests at heart

The FCA take a modern approach enabling the modern and innovative nature of Crowdfunding whilst keeping their priorities of protecting the Investor and nurturing business. Amongst other things, the FCA requires capital adequacy, client money protection, successor loan servicing, cancellation rights, disclosure requirements, dispute resolution and on-going reporting.

United States of America

'Prosper' was one of the first Crowdfunding platforms in the US. In those early days there was little regulation and there were few restrictions on Borrowers. Since 2008, the Securities and Exchange Commission (SEC) started to regulate Loan based Crowdfunding and trading stopped for a short while and some non-US companies left the US market altogether. The mission of the SEC is to protect Investors, maintain fair, orderly, and efficient markets, and facilitate capital formation.

The SEC treat Loan based Crowdfunding as 'securities' being sold to Investors by 'investment companies' offering 'investment advisors'. This is using existing regulation (often steeped in history) to regulate a very modern innovative finance industry. Added to this are any laws that individual states may have depending on the definition of the entities and where they operate. This leads to a complex system, leading some to openly criticise the US system and suggest it will struggle to be competitive in the global financial marketplace.

Europe

The European Banking Authority (EBA) has recommended the convergence of lending-based (Loan based) Crowdfunding regulation across the EU. One of the tasks of the EBA is to monitor new and existing financial activities and to adopt guidelines and recommendations with a view to promoting the safety and soundness of markets and convergence in regulatory practice.

According to the Authority, supervisory practices of Crowdfunding across the EU is desirable not only to avoid regulatory arbitrage, but also to ensure a level-playing field for all participants across the EU Single Market. The EBA explained that in these early stages of the development of Crowdfunding, regulatory convergence should be based on existing EU law, and recommended that EU legislators clarify its applicability.

Simple Crowdfunding Fact
According to Massollution's Crowdfunding Industry Report, Crowdfunding is on track to account for more funding than Venture Capital (VC) by 2016.

Just five years ago there was a relatively small market of 'early adopters' Crowdfunding online to the tune of a reported $880 million in 2010. Fast forward to today and we saw $16 billion crowdfunded in 2014, with 2015 estimated to grow to over $34 billion.

In comparison, the VC industry invests an average of $30 billion each year.

How To Succeed As A Borrower

"Dare to be different. Conformity is the enemy of innovation." – Albert Einstein

How To Select A Platform

Keep in mind that you are not alone in thinking of venturing into Crowdfunding. A good way to be noticed by potential Investors is to stand out and be different from the rest. Stand out from the crowd. Build your own network and create a compelling brand or project that contains a specific goal/plan for your Investors. Keep in mind that word of mouth is a powerful tool to spread the message and purpose of your brand. Select a Crowdfunding platform that lets you do this and feels right for your project.

Choosing which Crowdfunding platform to use is a very important decision. You shall need to consider a number of aspects before you decide which Crowdfunding platform is right for you.

Be in no doubt that many entrepreneurs, business owners, property investors and developers are operating successfully because of the funding they received from the variety of Crowdfunding platforms. It may now be your turn. Since every Crowdfunding site is not the same, decide carefully which platform to choose and weigh up the advantages and disadvantages of each platform. Make sure to list your project with only one platform and focus on the funding of the project once listed.

A list of Crowdfunding platforms can be found at the back of this book. Enjoy finding out about them!

General Tips

Make sure that your project is right for Crowdfunding. If you are not sure whether you will get funding, speak to the Crowdfunding platform and look at the projects they have on their site. Consider the amount your project needs and the way that backing will be delivered for your project.

Have a well thought out and solid plan for what you want to do. Study existing proposals on the site. Take the necessary time to produce a digestible plan that Investors will understand. Keep it engaging and simple. If you have a team, hold regular meetings to discuss the marketing of the project. If not, block out time for yourself to assess the marketing and adapt it as necessary depending upon how the pledges are progressing.

Make rewards enticing. If rewards will be part of your campaign, make sure that they are enticing so that receivers will be proud of them and others will want them. Also, have many levels of rewards so people can engage at different levels.

Have your pitch practised and polished. You never know when the opportunity to talk to a potential Investor will come. Whether it is one person or a room full. Remember to tell them your story as it is often easier to relate to stories. Prepare an 'elevator pitch'. This is usually no longer than a minute, and is generally the amount of time that you will spend with someone in an elevator. Be able to explain your project quickly and simply.

Talk to your network, friends and family before the project goes live on the Crowdfunding platform. A project that quickly gains pledges or already has some funding before it goes live is likely to attract more interest quickly as it already has some momentum and belief within the Investing community.   It is well worth making a list of everyone you know that may be interested in hearing about your project. Include everyone you can think of and when you speak to them, remind them they may have other friends and family who may also be interested and ask them to pass on your details. Keep a log of their response so that you know who to follow up, and when.

Bring out the 'you'. Investors tend to be interested in the person or company behind the project. Produce videos and be active on Social Media. It is important for Investors to see your passion and belief in the project.   Mention your background, relevant experience and showcase your successes. Don't forget that people will be watching your videos.   Consider your body language, dress sense and approach. It may be worth speaking to a media expert to get some tips

Don't be greedy and ask for more than you need. Keep it as low as your project can reasonably and safely manage and don't change your plan once created as this often damages confidence.

And finally, **look to inspire people** with your project or business idea.

Documentation

If you are planning to borrow funds, the Crowdfunding platform will need to process your application. You will be asked for a number of documents which may include financial and business documents. Not all Crowdfunding platforms are the same. Some shall ask for basic documents, some may ask for more detail. Some have very stringent tests, others are more relaxed. You should be prepared for the former.

Equity and Loan based Crowdfunding platforms tend to request the most information.

Investors will be concerned about the legality, expected return, loan process and the basis of your business idea or project. Also bear in mind that as a Borrower, you may be able to choose which Investors are right for your business idea or project if it is oversubscribed.

Below are the most common documents that Investors look to receive from potential Borrowers:

Business Plan

This is the most crucial part of the loan application and should give the Investor a clear insight into what the project or business idea is about. It should provide relevant background information, what the Borrower intends to do with the funds, the team involved and where the Borrower wants to take the project. The information should include a summary of the company, market analysis, marketing plans, and financial projections.

Financial Statements

These documents include bank statements, balance sheets, income statements, and cash flow projections. It should also include the Borrower's current financial position statement including accounts receivable and accounts payable. This will give the Investor an idea of the current financial stability of the Borrower.

Tax Returns

These reveal more financial information on the Borrower and will give Investors further insight into the financial acuity of the Borrower and profitability over recent years.

Legal Documents

These documents include business licenses, articles of incorporation, copies of contracts with third party companies, franchise agreements, and commercial leases. This will give Investors an idea of how legitimate and legally binding the business is. For instance, if the Borrower relies on a single supplier and does not have any secure contracts for their supply, this might be considered a risky situation. If the supplier decided not to supply the Borrower, the entire project may end there. An Investor may be well advised not to invest based upon the perceived risk in this instance.

Loan Repayment Plan

This repayment plan should include both the amount they intend to borrow and a description detailing how they intend to repay the business loan to the Investors. Borrowers should remember that Investors will always be on the lookout for 'what's in it for them'. The details of repayments, interest and any other reward must be set out clearly and be as attractive to an Investor as possible. But remember, never overstate what you will deliver on.

Security

With certain projects, security may be required in order to progress the loan. For example, if a Borrower was looking for funds to renovate a property, it is likely that the Crowdfunding platform will require a registered charge on the property until the funds are paid back.

If security is required for the project, the paperwork should be managed by the Crowdfunding platform who are then responsible for taking a charge (for security purposes) on behalf of the Investors. This paperwork will be in place before any funds are provided to the Borrower.

Additional Items

In addition to the above, Crowdfunding platforms will ask for personal information from a Borrower, including proof of ID, previous addresses, names used, their criminal record and educational background. Some Investors may even ask for an updated Resume from the Borrower. A Borrower does not have to give all the information asked for by an Investor, but if they don't, the Investor may be less likely to proceed.

Last but not least is the Credit Report. This can help improve the Borrower's chance of loan approval. If a Borrower has a very low credit score, Investors may consider them to be too high a risk. A Borrower may be able to counter balance this by offering higher levels of security or may perhaps want to delay listing their project until they improve their credit score.

It should be noted that not all of these documents are passed to the Investor. Some of these are required by the Crowdfunding platform to ensure that the Borrower and the project or business idea is viable.

Get Your Project Known

Once your project has been accepted on a Crowdfunding platform, you need to consider the marketing and promotion of your project. It is very important that you speak with the Crowdfunding platform in more detail to understand what you can and cannot do from a regulatory perspective. Donation based Crowdfunding has less regulation (if any) compared to that of Loan or Equity based Crowdfunding.

This promotion and marketing of your project is crucial and must be done correctly. A Crowdfunding campaign doesn't succeed on its own. As a Borrower, you need to be 100% committed in order to make it succeed. Part of this commitment is ensuring an excellent bid is prepared to give the project the best possible chance of being funded.

Create your marketing campaign calendar before you launch the campaign

Market your proposal wherever you can and to the correct audience. Schedule these activities to ensure that you have a consistent and coherent campaign. The campaign should build a story that reminds pledgers why your project is so investable. A one-off email is probably not enough to get you the funding needed unless you have already built up the interest using Public Relations (PR) or other means.

Be sure to have a plan in place before you launch your project. You need to keep the momentum going during the campaign and you need to be clear about your messaging so that prospective Investors see a story building rather than a 'scattergun approach' of marketing messages. Also consider a back-up plan. What are you going to do if the number of pledges look low? How can reach more people to promote your project?

Keep it relevant and simple

Ensure that your marketing content is right for your audience. A complicated spreadsheet of numbers may scare as many away as it attracts if your target market is not likely to be number focused. Consider the needs of your target market and whatever you do, keep the information clear and simple.

Make the most of communication channels

Use as many communication channels as possible. Facebook, Twitter, Instagram, Linked-In, You Tube, live events, TV, radio, blogs, flyers and leaflets, are all examples. The more you use, the wider your reach. You can also enter competitions for awards of related organisations which will help build credibility and give you more exposure. Note, if you are using video, keep them short and punchy and have follow-up communications that explain more.

Press releases and media coverage: messaging is key

Learn how to be detail oriented and make your story known at or even before the start of the campaign. Have a strategy for promotion of your project and if possible, pick a good journalist and media company to work with. It doesn't have to super expensive, the message should be clear and direct and targeted to your chosen market.

It also helps if you can have your campaign linked to a trending relevant news story, online video or topic. The message of your campaign should catch a person's interest. It could be something that can solve a problem or something that can interest the readers when they read or see your story.

So before making your story live ask yourself, "Will this be relevant to people when they read or see it?" Don't just use traditional marketing methods, make use of online channels including social media. Use whatever medium it takes to connect with your target market. Think outside the box and ask yourself continually "How can I promote this project so that more people will notice it?"

The storyline of your campaign

Blogs are the storyline of your campaign. List down the things that are relevant to your campaign so that it is easier to write your blog. Only include the things that matter so that you can avoid time wastage. Explain this in detail, step by step. This can then be used throughout your campaign, from initial fundraising activities through to project completion.

Always remember to be able to fully deliver the purpose of your campaign. Targeting the right audience and being specific to your objectives. Don't waste your time reaching out to wrong people.

Success breeds success

Model your campaigns on other successful award-winning or competition winning campaigns. Evaluate the best and use those lessons yourself. Follow their strategies and learn from their approach. You already have the idea; learn from other successful projects how to announce yours to the world.

Optimise your campaign with Search Engine Optimisation (SEO)

If you're creating a web based blog for your campaign, it is necessary for people to find it. Ensure that your blog or project ranks highly with search engines so that people can find it when searching online. Do whatever it takes and optimise your content using keywords etc. so that potential Investors can find you.

Crowdfunding does take time and is perhaps more proactive than getting a bank loan. It can often be more rewarding though.

What You Should Ask As A Borrower

A Borrower wants to ensure that the Crowdfunding platform they launch their project on is well run, legitimate and trustworthy. The following are questions a Borrower should consider asking the platform before launching their project. And remember, asking the question is only the start. You then need to ensure you receive answers to each question, backed with documentary evidence where available, and then to read and check the replies. Are they correct and sufficient? Do they reveal areas of doubt or conjecture that prompt further questions? If so, ask them. Your project will be tied to that platform once launched. Choose a poor platform and your Crowdfunding project may fail and your project be delayed for months or lost altogether.

1. Are you regulated by the FCA? (UK – Equity or Loan)
2. Do you have any warnings or any disciplinary history recorded against the platform?
3. Do you have separate client or escrow facilities for money transfer?
4. Are you or your platform currently under investigation?
5. How does the platform work and what are your responsibilities?

6. Do you need security and if so, what will you consider?
7. What is the maximum term of the loan that you will accept? (Loan)
8. What is the minimum term of the loan that you will accept? (Loan)
9. Is there an entry and exit fee?
10. How are the fees broken down and can you provide full details?
11. What interest rates will I need to pay? (Loan)
12. When do I need to pay the interest and can I defer to the end of the project? (Loan)
13. What happens if I cannot pay the loan or the interest payments back? (Loan)
14. What if I change my mind?
15. What happens if I don't reach my target goal?
16. How long does it take from approval to get the project launched?
17. What happens if want to pay back the loan before the end of the term? (Loan)
18. What happens if I need further funds?
19. What are the risks for a Borrower?

Simple Crowdfunding Fact

Based upon 'Kickstarter' research of 686 top overfunded projects, 93% of funding was raised by campaigns that were started on weekdays. Furthermore, overfunded projects launched on Tuesdays and Wednesdays brought in over half (53%) of all the money raised.

How To Succeed As An Investor

"We have to think of new ways to unlock capital for the business that can address social challenges, while still protecting investors from bad investments." – Anthony Bugg-Levine

As an Investor, you want to ensure your money that you may be investing is as safe as the investment project allows. First of all, you need to check that the Crowdfunding platform is legitimate, creditworthy and trustworthy. After all, your money will be passed through them and they shall have complete control over it at that time.

The Different Types Of Returns

Interest Payments

This is based upon a percentage return being agreed when the project is proposed. Interest payments can be made at either regular intervals, such as monthly or quarterly, or at the end of the term when the original loan amount is repaid.

Equity

This means shares or part ownership of the project or company that you are investing in. How long you are tied to the company or project before you can realise your gains is agreed at the beginning of the project. If the project or company increases in value, so may the value of your shares. If the project or company does not do as well as expected and their value goes down, then so may the value of your shares. If the project or company fails, then your investment could be worth nothing.

Rewards

Returns from these types of Crowdfunding projects are not shares or a percentage return of interest payments. These types of Crowdfund opportunities tend to offer an item or service in exchange for the investment. These include early editions of products, membership deals and personalised goods such as personalised games where Investors are the characters.

How To Select A Crowdfunding Platform

As an Investor, you want to ensure that the Crowdfunding platform that you are investing your money through is entirely legitimate, legal and 'above board'. If you are looking for Loan based or Equity Crowdfunding in the UK, then these activities are regulated by the Financial Conduct Authority (FCA). You should check that the company you are looking to invest through is registered AND licenced to carry out the activities that you want and it claims to offer. Note that you can also check with the FCA for any disciplinary history the Crowdfunding platform may have.

All communication from the Crowdfunding platform should be clear and concise. They should also make clear any risks involved with investing through their site.

It is worth noting that the FCA has introduced a Capital Adequacy Requirement which means that the Crowdfunding platform must keep it's own cash in reserve in case of difficulty. How much depends upon the size and turnover of the company.

Paperwork

In order to quality as an Investor, there will be checks that the Crowdfunding platform will perform before you are able to lend – especially for Loan based or Equity based projects. The level of checks will be dependent upon the Crowdfunding platform and will typically be correlated to the amount that you are looking to invest.

The Crowdfunding platform will ask for personal information including proof of ID, and proof of funds. These are typically required by the Crowdfunding platform so that they can fulfil their Anti Money Laundering (AML) duties. They will also ask you to confirm that you fully understand the risks of investing in Crowdfund projects before they will allow you to pledge.

To Secure Or Not To Secure

Some Crowdfunding platforms will require security from the Borrowers in order to further protect Investor funds. Whilst this does not guarantee that an Investor will receive their funds back if a project goes sour, there is a better chance that the funds will be recoverable. An obvious example of when security may exist is in a Crowdfunded property project. If a Borrower has a piece of land and wishes to raise finance for the development and build, the Crowdfunding platform will look to take a registered charge on the land. The value of the land must be enough to cover the original amount borrowed, fees associated with liquidating the asset and also Crowdfunding platform fees in order to achieve this.

It is always worth having the security / non-security conversation with any Crowdfunding platform that you are looking to invest through – especially for large sums of finance!

Promotion

Even though you are a potential Investor, there are still good reasons for you to ensure that the project you are hoping to invest in is promoted well. The main reason is that if the project is not promoted well, it is less likely that the required level of funding shall be reached. If a project doesn't reach its funding target, its attempt at Crowdfunding will not succeed. If the project doesn't go ahead, then your potential investment opportunity will not get off the ground.

As an Investor, you can and should do all that you can to promote the project that you are interested in. First of all, you should check with the Crowdfunding platform about what regulations may affect the promotion of the project that you are interested in. Do any regulations restrict its promotion, or are there any other guidelines which the Crowdfunding platform can advise you about?

If there are no restrictions, as a potential Investor, you would do well to bring the project to the attention of all your contacts, using all the media channels previously mentioned in the section for Borrowers, to ensure the nature of the project is broadcast to as wide an audience as possible.

What You Should Ask As An Investor

Investors should always do their research on the Crowdfunding platform as well as on each project and Borrower. These are certain questions that can and should be asked. This list is not exhaustive and should a question occur to you, ask it! If you do not receive an answer, or a straight answer, beware. You should ensure that you trust the platform. If you don't, it may be worth considering others before making your final decision.

1. Are you regulated by the FCA? (UK Equity and Loan)
2. Do you have any warnings or any disciplinary history recorded against the platform?
3. Do you have separate client or escrow facilities for money transfer?
4. Are you or your platform currently under investigation?
5. Is my investment secured and if so, how?
6. What happens if the interest payments stop or the project or business idea goes wrong?
7. What happens if the capital is not returned to me on time?
8. How long will it take to recover funds if needed?
9. How long will my money be tied up for?
10. Can you invest my money for me?
11. What are the risks associated with this investment?
12. What happens if I need to access my investment before the term is up?
13. What return will I get for my investment?
14. What is the platform's investment criteria, and do you need to be a 'Sophisticated Investor' to invest?
15. What checks do you perform on Investors (if any)?

Simple Crowdfunding Fact

A Surrey home listed on Property Partner was snapped up in 35 minutes. 126 Investors contributed a total of £212,900 towards the deal.

Crowdfunding Success Stories

"People will always be your most important asset." – Chris Cunningham

There have been some wonderful Crowdfunding successes over the years. Here are some of our favourites:

Squishyforts

Ross Currie, from Perth Australia launched a campaign for Squishyforts. Initially he wanted $25,000, but he managed to get the fund up to $67,000.

Many of us have built forts or houses out of cushions in our younger days, some still do and some still enjoy building cushion forts with their children today.

Australian Entrepreneur Ross Currie heard about a blog by the architect Andrew van Leeuwen that grew so popular that it overwhelmed his server, on the end he had to remove the article. The article was about pillow forts. Andrew had found a subject that many people had fond memories of, and were keen to read about today.

Many blogs and articles will go into the structural properties of different types of pillow and blankets and any other object that can be used to build a fort, they also go into the luxury elements of modern forts. Architects, builders, scientists and children of all ages can really get in to the concept if they haven't already.

Ross built a series of kits that comprised of cushions that have magnets helping you to build a fort with them. People found storage an issue and the breakthrough came when Ross designed the cushions into an Ottoman that could be part of the existing furniture. Ross had seen an issue through prototyping and developed his product to overcome it.

Ross offered discount vouchers to early backers and kept his backers and potential backers informed of progress. Squishyforts began shipping in June 2015. Ross continues to keep backers informed about his customers enjoying squishyforts.

www.squishyforts.com

Lovespace

With storage space being increasingly difficult to find, Lovespace saw a gap in the market. They also thought about the process of a customer getting their items for storage to and from the storage area. Lovespace saw a need and decided to address it.

In June 2014 Lovespace were able to fund their start-up using crowdfunding with 259 Investors. They secured £600,000 in just 24 hours going on to raise £1,562,960 in 12 days with an Equity based Crowdfund giving 28.49% equity to the Investors between them. Lovespace did so well they were awarded 'Crowdfunded Business of the Year' at the Start-up Awards in 2014 against some big competition.

Brett Akker launched Lovespace in 2012, by April 2015 they have stored over 10,000 boxes for 2,000 customers and continue to grow by 50 customers a day.

Some traditional finance houses have suggested that further finance would be hard for 'crowd' financed business to expand. Love space has since gained £1.1 million of private investment to push their growth further, showing that Crowdfunding works well with solid business ideas.

www.lovespace.co.uk

Pebble

Pebble is a company that worked to develop smart watches. The founder needed to raise funds and decided to try and do this using Crowdfunding.

An astonishing 68,929 Investors decided to back the project, and in doing so pledged a massive $10.3 million, which was the highest ever at that time.

In July 2013 the 'Pebble Watch' was released and sold out in 5 days.

Now the company employs 130 people and Pebble continues to use Crowdfunding to raise funds and bring new smart watches to the market. They also now partner with many larger, more traditional companies.

Pebble launched a new project in February 24th 2015 and in March 28th 2015 (just over a month later!) had raised $20,338,986 with 78,471 backers. Crowdfunding can be immensely powerful once a project captures the imagination!

www.getpebble.com

Studio Neat

The number of smartphones in use is on the rise, and most have a camera. Built in camera technology is progressing rapidly, so a need for a way to mount a smartphone like a standalone camera has appeared.

Studio Neat launched the 'Glif', a small device that can prop up your smart phone for viewing or reading. More importantly it allows individuals to attach their smartphone to a tripod, just like a traditional camera.

The project launched on October 4th 2010 with a modest goal of $10,000, with the hope of selling 500 of them. 24 hours later, they had doubled their goal and by the end of the 30 day campaign, they had raised $137,417 with 5,273 backers. By December 10th 2010 the Glifs were shipping to backers and customers.

Six months later, they launched a second campaign. For the first two days of the campaign, they tried something unique, offering a 'pay what you want' model, raising nearly $50,000 within 48 hours. By the end of the campaign, they had raised $134,236.

www.studioneat.com

Safe House Hostel

Daniel Wimpelberg (Dan) from Cardiff found a building that had been empty for many years. Developers and other potential Investors were finding it difficult to do anything with the property as it had listed features.

He got some like-minded people together and agreed on the way forward. They were granted planning permission and managed to get enough funding to convert the building into an amazing hostel.

As with many building projects there were a few surprises and extra funding was needed. Dan was able to use Crowdfunding to get the funding he needed and get the hostel up and running.

Dan had a $10,000 target and managed to get $13,303 from 52 funders. The generosity and power of crowdfunding worked well here to look after an historic building and give travellers a safe and cost effective place to stay.

www.safehousehostel.co.uk

Easy Property

Easy Property is an online letting agent. Rob Ellice worked with Stelios Haji-Ionnou and took the traditional estate agent approach and rebuilt it as a more efficient modern online offering.

Easy Property had an initial target of £1,000,000 and raised £1,358,680 (135 %) from 376 Investors in late 2014. Easy Property is so popular that funding was stopped though Investors were still invited to register their interest should funding options start again in the future for this company.

This shows how Crowdfunding can raise your profile among Investors for future funding, not just the funding you are looking for now.

www.easyproperty.com

Oculus Rift – VR Headset

Oculus is one of the biggest Crowdfunding success stories of all time. They started with a vision of delivering incredible, affordable, and ubiquitous consumer virtual reality to the world. They've come a long way: from foam core prototypes built in a garage to an incredible community of active and talented developers with more than 75,000 development kits ordered.

In order to raise finance, Oculus used the Kickstarter platform and within a 30 day campaign, raised $2,437,429 with 9,522 backers. The Oculus team went on to raise additional investment capital and was acquired by Facebook. The $2 billion acquisition was controversial and many Crowdfunding backers that contributed to the Oculus campaign expressed their desire to benefit from the company's success since they were the first supporters of the company.

www.oculus.com/en-us/rift

Simple Crowdfunding Fact

One of the first modern day Crowdfunding projects can be traced back to Dr. Mohammad Yunus in 1976. Yunus gave low-income individuals the chance of getting a loan from a bank. He began by loaning $27 to 42 women in Bangladesh to start their own businesses. Seven years and thousands of success stories later, Yunus' loan program became Grameen Bank.

Those thousands of stories have since turned into over 8 million Borrowers that are able to flourish with the given resources. These revolutionary actions brought Yunus and Grameen Bank a Nobel Peace Prize in 2006.

What Next?

"There is a growing movement afoot to revolutionise banking, investing and giving by using technology to simplify the links between those who want to invest money and those who need it. Crowdfunding and peer-to-peer finance are at the vanguard of this movement." – Stian Westlake

In recent years Crowdfunding has grown from being an innovative concept to a multi-billion dollar industry and in the UK is expected to be a multi-billion pound industry this year (2015). Industries from gaming to finance, from property to research, use Crowdfunding to grow their businesses and bring to market products and services that may otherwise not have got funded. Many Borrowers who have had bad experiences with banks welcome such an open and transparent alternative source of finance. They like the ability to continue running their business without a VC company or Angel Investor seemingly taking control. And Investors are also intrigued by the opportunity of better returns.

In the UK and the US, regulation is gathering pace and making the Crowdfunding marketplace a safer place to be. Existing business and financial institutions are also getting on the band wagon and starting to buy up existing Crowdfunding platforms, whilst some of the larger Crowdfunding platforms are attracting large investors for themselves and IPO'ing (Initial Public Offering).

Crowdfunding is already helping businesses get funding where banks have refused to fund. In time, it may be the case that Crowdfunding will replace 'traditional finance options' for some business owners, entrepreneurs and property developers. As for Angel Investors and Venture Capitalists, Crowdfunding is taking its place alongside them.

There is a proven track record of Loan based Crowdfunding, showing returns and successes for both Borrowers and Investors. Equity based Crowdfunding is starting to show successes as well, and confidence is growing in this developing sector. This will help confidence with small Investors as well as larger institutions. Some of the success is it's ability to leverage the openness and speed of the internet and Social Media channels. It also allows Borrowers and Investors the opportunity to have the project scrutinised, often, and by a large number of people. There can be safety in numbers. If a large number of people have looked at the project and don't like it, for whatever reason, it may be a very good prompt to both the Borrower and Investors that something is indeed wrong with the project. Conversely, if the take up rate is high and pledges are pouring in, maybe the project is right for the market and more likely to succeed. The project's response almost becomes its own market research!

Should a Borrower have demonstrably strong support in the early stages of the project that is itself is a good indicator which can support the process of finding other Investors.

The Crowdfunding world has moved from its infancy stage into a more settled regime and is now under the guidance and regulation of governing bodies. The types of businesses and individuals that look to Crowdfunding for investment are expanding. Traditionally, technology, food or gaming sectors did really well on Crowdfunding sites. Many other sectors are now looking to the crowd, and the crowd is enjoying the diversity that this provides.

As Crowdfunding grows and gains traction it is increasingly leveraged as a real alternative to traditional finance options, whereas before, it may have been considered a last resort. Crowdfunding's open approach to information sharing about the project and the people behind it brings a personal and human aspect to an otherwise fairly dull finance market.

There is so much opportunity out there and the most amazing products, developments and services are coming to market because of crowd backing. As an Investor, you have the opportunity to pick and choose the projects that most resonate with you and deliver the best returns or rewards. As a Borrower, you now have access to potentially millions of Investors. On both sides, the opportunity is massive. Embrace it!

Simple Crowdfunding Fact

Global crowdfunding experienced accelerated growth in 2014, expanding by 167 percent to reach $16.2 billion raised, up from $6.1 billion in 2013. In 2015, the industry is set to more than double once again, on its way to raising $34.4 billion. - Massolution's Crowdfunding Industry Report

Resources

*"When you give everyone a voice and give people power;
the system usually ends up in a really good place." –
Mark Zuckerberg*

There are many useful sources of information if you are keen to find out more about Crowdfunding. The below is not a comprehensive list of Crowdfunding platforms or Associations and there are many more out there.   However, the below will get you started on your Crowdfunding journey.

Regulatory And Association Websites

www.fca.org.uk
www.fca.org.uk/consumers/financial-services-
products/investments/types-of-investment/crowdfunding
www.moneyadviceservice.org.uk
www.moneyadviceservice.org.uk/en/articles/peer-to-peer-loans
www.ukcfa.org.uk
www.p2pfa.info
www.nesta.org.uk/project/crowdfunding
www.financial-ombudsman.org.uk

www.ec.europa.eu
www.ec.europa.eu/finance/general-
policy/crowdfunding/index_en.htm
www.eba.europa.eu
www.eba.europa.eu/-/eba-recommends-convergence-of-lending-
based-crowdfunding-regulation-across-the-eu

www.sec.gov
www.sec.gov/news/pressrelease/2015-49.html
www.nlcfa.org

Some Of Our Favourite Crowdfunding Platforms

Below are some of our favourite Crowdfunding platforms. They include Rewards based platforms such as 'Kickstarter', Donation based platforms such as 'Causes' and Loan based platforms such as 'Simple Backing'. Some are further split by industry such as Technology, Music, Property or Publishing.

1.   www.Simplebacking.co.uk
2.   www.Kickstarter.com
3.   www.Indiegogo.com
4.   www.Crowdcube.com
5.   www.Fundable.com
6.   www.Gofundme.com
7.   www.Lendingclub.com
8.   www.Seedrs.com
9.   www.Razoo.com
10.   www.Causes.com
11.   www.Crowdrise.com
12.   www.Rockethub.com
13.   www.Justgiving.com/Crowdfunding
14.   www.Fundingcircle.com/uk
15.   www.Artistshare.com/v4
16.   www.Techmoola.com
17.   www.Pubslush.com
18.   www.Fundmyventure.co.uk
19.   www.Giveforward.com

Simple Crowdfunding Fact

Crowdfunding will create 2.2 million new jobs by 2020. 1 job is created for every £23,371 invested / donated – Funding Tree

About The Authors

"As long as you are going to be thinking anyway, think big." – Donald Trump

Davin Poonwassie

Davin's background is in data and databases, being unusually qualified in the three most used databases, MSSQL, MySQL and Oracle. He has been providing Database Management support and consultancy to a number of clients, both in the UK and overseas. He is also a British Computer Society Chartered IT Professional.

In May 2015, Davin became a full time entrepreneur, focusing on the Simple Backing Crowdfunding business that he co-founded with Atuksha back in 2013.

In addition to this, Davin is a keen property investor. His first taste of property investing came when he was at University. Davin Joint

Ventured with his brother to buy an investment property that Davin and his friends could live in. This was then parked until 2003 when Davin started building his portfolio, investing in Kent. He now has a small portfolio of properties in Kent, South Wales and the French Alps.

Atuksha Poonwassie

Atuksha is the owner of Focus 2020 Ltd. Since May 2000 when the company was formed, Atuksha has been providing Customer Relationship Management guidance and support to businesses across many industries and across all regions. Atuksha enjoys exploring and resolving customer engagement challenges. She is passionate about working with businesses to increase profits whilst building better long-term relationships. She believes that a directed communication plan, regardless of channel, is vital to maintaining a loyal customer and prospect base.

She is also a keen property investor and has also project managed significant builds and bought empty properties back to life, creating homes for families. She is a keen Crowdfunder and loves this exciting and (fairly) new marketplace.

About Simple Backing

Simple Backing is a Crowdfunding platform that specialises in Peer to Peer lending. It connects Investors with Borrowers through property projects and smart business ideas to the benefit of all involved.

The Simple Backing team are all property investors and / or developers and are successful business owners. They are passionate about what they do and love to see new business ideas and property projects come to life.

To find out more, visit our website: **www.SimpleBacking.co.uk**

Simple Crowdfunding Fact
The number of firms operating Loan-Based Crowdfunding (Peer to Peer Lending), or seeking to enter this sector has increased from 50 in April 2014 to 57 by the end of 2014. A further 112 applications for licences have since been received by the FCA – Financial Conduct Authority

Our Final Thoughts

"First, think. Second, believe. Third, dream. And finally, dare." – Walt Disney

We hope that this book has given you a thirst to find out more about Crowdfunding. There is so much information to share, but with more platforms coming online and regulations changing frequently, it is virtually impossible to share detailed content in this book.

Our goal is to give you a flavour of what Crowdfunding is about and to inspire you to find out more about this growing financial platform. There is SO much opportunity that this marketplace brings and we truly believe that projects, products and services that may otherwise have been overlooked now have the opportunity to shine. If you have a need for funding, there has been no better time to attain it. You have the opportunity to gather and grow a group of enthusiasts interested in your project's success.

Enjoy the opportunity and the journey – not only is Crowdfunding destined to grow exponentially in the coming years, it is also SO much fun.

The future belongs to the crowd!

Simple Crowdfunding Fact
The Crowdfunding industry worldwide has grown over 1000% in the last 5 years (to end 2014).

Simple Crowdfunding's Success

Within a week of launching the book on Kindle, 'Simple Crowdfunding' hit Amazon #1 Bestseller in its category, something that we are very proud of. We are also fortunate to have our book seen in many places including: